I0413124

NIST Internal Report 6660

Workshop on Quantitative Tools for Condition Assessment of Aging Infrastructure

May 4-5, 2010

Boulder, Colorado

Editors:
Jessica Terry
Tom Siewert
David McColskey
Ward Johnson
Materials Reliability Division
Materials Science and Engineering Laboratory

William Luecke
Mark Iadicola
Dat Duthinh
Metallurgy Division
Materials Science and Engineering Laboratory

October 2010

U. S. Department of Commerce
Gary Locke, Secretary

National Institute of Standards and Technology
Patrick D. Gallagher, Director

Table of Contents

Executive Summary

The Quantitative Tools for Condition Assessment of Aging Infrastructure workshop was held May 4-5, 2010, to prioritize measurement and standards needs relative to inspection, maintenance, repair, and replacement of the Nation's physical infrastructure. The workshop focused on steel bridges, and the principal stakeholders in attendance included bridge owners, manufacturers of inspection equipment, and government and academic researchers. Discussion themes included (1) uncertainty in inspection data, (2) advanced sensors, (3) behavior of connections, and (4) mechanical response of materials.

Many measurement and standards needs were raised and discussed during breakout discussions, from which forty-three suggested research topics were deemed to be of high enough interest to be considered by the entire workshop. Twenty-three topics were selected and ranked by stakeholder vote to be of highest priority to the bridge community. The top eleven topics were:

- Methods for accurate, cost-effective field measurement of absolute stress or strain and any neccessary reference artifacts.
- Simple and robust methods for rapid load rating of bridges.
- Analysis and validation of existing and new crack arrest strategies, especially for distortion-induced cracks.
- Methods to determine the location, size, and condition of reinforcing steel in hardened concrete.
- Standardized methods for accelerated life-testing of embedded sensors for structural health monitoring.
- Standard reference specimens and calibration services to validate nondestructive inspection techniques and instruments.
- Improved documentary standards for visual inspection methods and probability of detection.
- Standard test apparatus for qualification of new sensors and instrumentation for structural health monitoring.
- Critical data on the behavior of high performance steels and connections at high temperatures (400 °C to 1100 °C).
- Validation of reduced-scale testing approaches to supplement full-scale testing.
- Critical data on the fatigue resistance of bolted and riveted connections, especially when loose or exposed to high temperatures.

More details on these and other suggested topics can be found in the following report. This information will be used by NIST for internal program planning and will form the basis for development of new collaborations across organizations to address tasks of mutual interest.

Acronyms

AASHTO	American Association of State Highway and Transportation Officials
ABC	accelerated bridge construction
AE	acoustic emission
ASR	alkali-silica reaction
BFRL	NIST Building and Fire Research Laboratory, after Fiscal Year 2010 referred to as the NIST Engineering Laboratory
BMS	bridge management systems
DOT	Department of Transportation
EMAT	electromagnetic-acoustic transducers
FEA	finite-element analysis
FEM	finite-element model
FHWA	Federal Highway Administration
GPR	ground penetrating radar
HPS	high-performance steels
LRFD	load and resistance factor design
MEMS	micro-electro-mechanical systems
MSE	mechanically stabilized earth
MSEL	NIST Materials Science and Engineering Laboratory, after Fiscal Year 2010 referred to as the NIST Materials Measurement Laboratory
NBIS	National Bridge Inspection Standards
NCHRP	National Cooperative Highway Research Program
NDE	nondestructive evaluation
NIST	National Institute of Standards and Technology
PAUT	phased-array ultrasonic testing
POD	probability of detection
SHM	structural health monitoring
TIP	NIST Technology Innovation Program
TRB	Transportation Research Board
UT	ultrasonic technology

Introduction

Recent high-visibility failures of aging structures in the US infrastructure have highlighted the need for improved technology and measurement science to better predict the remaining life of other critical structures. [1, 2] Since limited funds are available for repair and replacement, the Nation must carefully prioritize these activities. These critical issues led to the organization of this workshop, which was focused on measurement needs for condition assessment of bridges.

The workshop, "Quantitative Tools for Condition Assessment of Aging Infrastructure," was held May 4-5, 2010, at the NIST laboratory in Boulder, Colorado. The goal of the workshop was to sharpen the focus of NIST's programs by matching the measurement technology capabilities of MSEL, in conjunction with other NIST organizations (Building and Fire Research Laboratory and the Technology Innovation Program), with existing technology gaps in the bridge industry, specifically for assessing the condition of bridges to prioritize their repair and replacement. The workshop brought together 30 bridge stakeholders representing four categories: bridge owners, manufacturers of inspection equipment, and government researchers, and academic researchers. The stakeholders identified areas that prioritize measurement and standards needs relative to inspection, maintenance, repair, and replacement of the Nation's physical infrastructure. The workshop began with several keynote presentations to frame the topics. After the keynote presentations, the participants developed and ranked a list of potential research activities in breakout sessions that focused on four subject areas: (1) uncertainty in inspection data, (2) advanced sensors, (3) behavior of connections, and (4) mechanical response of materials. The workshop concluded with all the stakeholders reconvening to develop a consensus on the most critical technologies. The agenda is included as Appendix II.

The stakeholders in attendance were leaders in the field or their chosen delegates, and were drawn primarily from contacts developed by NIST researchers at past bridge events such as the American Association of State Highway and Transportation Officials (AASHTO) July 2009 meeting, the Transportation Research Board's (TRB) January 2010 meeting, and visits to various universities. The NIST workshop provided a unique venue for comparison of NIST mission and MSEL's expertise with critical research topics identified by these stakeholders. These proceedings document the discussed topics without comment and constitute no specific commitment by MSEL or NIST to pursue research in these areas. Technical conclusions of the workshop were also highlighted in a presentation on research needs at the AASHTO Subcommittee on Bridges and Structures Annual Meeting, May 23-27 in Sacramento, California [Friedland 2010].

The four breakout sessions were led by researchers with experience in the specific subject areas. For

---

[1] http://www.infrastructurereportcard.org/

[2] http://www.ntsb.gov/dockets/Highway/HWY07MH024/404995.pdf

each session, a NIST representative recorded the discussions and provided some guidance on whether the ideas would fit within the NIST mission. A brief background for each breakout session is presented below, and the results of the ensuing discussions are presented later in this report. Discussion of some pertinent current research is also included.

1. Uncertainty in Inspection Data – Session chair: George Hearn, Session recorder: Jessica Terry

    Goal: Reduce the uncertainty in the data developed during inspections and periodic NDE investigations

    Background – Bridge inspection is a predominantly subjective undertaking, and relies heavily on inspector training and experience, as well as agency preferences. The National Bridge Inspection Standards (NBIS) stipulate maximum intervals for routine, underwater inspections as well as inspections of fracture-critical bridges. Routine and underwater inspections intervals are influenced by agency preferences for frequency as well as extensions subject to FHWA approval. Inspection and repair costs could be optimized if a bridge's remaining life could be quantified through specific testing, tools, and measurement technology. This topic is currently under investigation with FHWA's NCHRP Project 12-82, "Developing Reliability-Based Bridge Inspection Practices." The project's goal is to match the inspection cycle with the need for inspection, not just the calendar. Development of tools for in-depth and special inspections that locate damage that is undetected during visual inspections may be limited to certain classes of bridges. These classes of bridges may be the type where expensive replacement motivates maximizing the bridge's life span. NDE tools have been developed to assist in bridge monitoring, but in many cases their application has been limited by complexity, availability, cost, and lack of guidance on field deployment. Certain methods can provide false readings (both positive and negative) due to improper calibration. An opportunity exists to expand the use of these advanced tools if their error and uncertainty could be reduced and their output could be simplified.

2. Advanced Sensors – Session chair: Steven Lovejoy; Session recorder: Ward Johnson

    Goal: Development and certification of practical SHM sensors

    Background - Continuous SHM of bridges with permanently mounted sensors is now widely viewed as offering the potential of characterizing structural degradation in a more objective, complete, and timely manner than the periodic inspections that are currently employed. Although some new bridges are instrumented for SHM, approaches for sensor design and function are not well established. Methods of network integration and information processing are also not standardized.

3. Behavior of Connections – Session chair: Karl Frank; Session recorder: William Luecke

    Goal: Improved prediction of actual performance of steel bridges through a better understanding of the behavior of connections

    Background - The actual performance and safety of structural connections designed by use of simple empirical formulas are difficult to assess in the presence of initial imperfections in geometry or materials. Further scrutiny is needed, especially in the case of structures without

7

redundancies in the load path. Finite-element modeling (FEM) is a powerful tool to design a single connection or (through simplifications) an entire structure. Currently, however, it is too computationally complex to model an entire structure down to the level of a rivet, bolt, or weld, but it is in these details that the performance and critical failure conditions of the connections lie. Further refinement of models by adding fatigue, corrosion, realistic failure criteria, and the effects of fire for the materials at these critical links is also not routinely possible. To address these deficiencies, measurement of bridge connection degradation mechanisms and the resulting effect on performance is necessary. These measurements and observations must then be converted into simple but accurate numerical models that capture the current state of the overall system. Once established, these models could provide the necessary foundation for more accurately determining system safety during operation and could aid in establishing guidelines for sensor specifications and placement strategies for improved bridge inspection. Current collaboration with FHWA is shown in the recent output from NCHRP Project 12-84 "Gusset Plate Connections for Steel Bridges" [Hartman 2010].

4. Mechanical Response of Materials – Session chair: Theodore Zoli; Session recorder: Dat Duthinh

   Goal: Quantify effects of environmental degradation, normal service loading, occasional accidental loading, design errors and extreme events such as fire or impact, on failure potential

   Background - Structural engineers design for expected service conditions by use of well established, validated design rules backed by decades of experience, and for accidental loading by use of a limited probabilistic method- load and resistance factor design (LRFD)-. However, the in-service performance of structural materials under extreme conditions caused by fire, explosion, impact, and natural disasters, especially in aged, degraded conditions typical of the US infrastructure, is not well addressed in the design codes. Possible exceptions are in the structural response to hurricane and earthquake loadings and structural responses, which have attracted significant research funding for many years. Design errors may also cause dangerous conditions under normal service loads. Furthermore, next-generation materials intended as replacements may respond in unexpected ways, or their mechanical properties may not have been fully explored. In addition, most structural models assume average material properties (*e.g.*, tensile strength of steel) based on data acquired at ambient temperatures under specifically defined load conditions – in fact, fire is not a design consideration for bridges at all! Accurate estimation of the residual factor of safety for aged structures under normal and "extreme" conditions is critical to prioritizing the need for repair or replacement.

The breakout sessions started with additional presentations by stakeholders, followed by development of a list of potential research topics for NIST. The breakout sessions lasted two hours in the afternoon of the first day and another hour in the morning of the second day, which allowed the stakeholders to discuss potential research topics and their fit to the NIST mission and capabilities.

The top five to seven ideas from each breakout session were brought back to a plenary session. Here, the stakeholders heard explanations of all the ideas, and voted on their importance. The votes of each of the four categories of participants (bridge owners, manufacturers of inspection equipment, and government and academic researchers) were kept separate to identify any group preferences. Based on the final vote in the plenary session, recommendations for the eleven highest priority areas of research include:

- Methods for accurate, cost-effective field measurement of absolute stress or strain and any neccessary reference artifacts.
- Simple and robust methods for rapid load rating of bridges.
- Analysis and validation of existing and new crack arrest strategies, especially for distortion-induced cracks.
- Methods to determine the location, size, and condition of reinforcing steel in hardened concrete.
- Standardized methods for accelerated life-testing of embedded sensors for structural health monitoring.
- Standard reference specimens and calibration services to validate nondestructive inspection techniques and instruments.
- Improved documentary standards for visual inspection methods and probability of detection.
- Standard test apparatus for qualification of new sensors and instrumentation for structural health monitoring.
- Critical data on the behavior of high performance steels and connections at high temperatures (400 $^{\circ}$C to 1100 $^{\circ}$C).
- Validation of reduced-scale testing approaches to supplement full-scale testing.
- Critical data on the fatigue resistance of bolted and riveted connections, especially when loose or exposed to high temperatures.

Details on the voting breakdown are tabulated in Appendix III.

While this research list will help NIST determine the direction of research projects, the magnitude of the tasks is too great for NIST to complete by itself in a timely fashion. Collaborators and partners will be necessary to leverage NIST efforts.

Keynote Presentations

Five keynote presentations were given as broad overviews that would provide general guidance and background to the four breakout sessions[3]:

1. Frank Gayle (Metallurgy Division Chief, NIST), *NIST Overview: Organization and Mission*

This presentation described the structure of NIST, its mission, and the mission of MSEL.

---

[3] The slides from the keynote and breakout session presentations can be found in Appendix I

2.   Stephanie Hooker (Materials Reliability Division Chief, NIST), *Overview of MSEL Plan: Quantitative Tools for Condition Assessment of Aging Infrastructure*

This presentation described MSEL's proposed plan to address the measurement needs in our aging infrastructure.

3.   Ian Friedland (Technical Director, Bridges and Structures R&D, FHWA), *Bridge Research: Current Issues and Future Opportunities*

This presentation summarized the mission and capabilities of the FHWA and suggested how NIST could help to address critical research needs in highway infrastructure.

4.   Dan Frangopol (Fazlur R. Khan Endowed Chair of Structural Engineering and Architecture, Lehigh University), *Assessing and Predicting the Performance of Bridges to Prioritize their Repair and Replacement: Accomplishments and Challenges*

This presentation was an academic perspective on the multi-faceted incorporation of reliability and optimization of bridge performance assessment, with comments on remaining challenges.

5.   Alex Wilson (Customer Service Technical Manager, ArcelorMittal), American Iron and Steel Institute (AISI) Bridge Task Force, *Overview and measurement needs that MSEL might fill*

This presentation was a material supplier's perspective of the research needs in infrastructure.

Breakout Sessions
I. Uncertainty in Inspection Data
A. Introduction
The majority of topics discussed in the Uncertainty in Inspection Information breakout session fell within three categories: accessibility, validation, and evaluation.

Accessibility refers to the need to effectively inspect (determine condition or behavior of) bridge elements that cannot be visually inspected. Non-visible elements include concrete reinforcing steel bars, prestressing strands (post-tensioned and pre-tensioned), some underwater foundation elements, steel pins, multiple plies of built-up material, joints in pre-fabricated structures, certain box girders, rock bolts, and steel straps embedded in mechanically stabilized earth (MSE) walls. Because inspections are performed primarily with visual techniques, many of the discussions related to the accessibility of various bridge elements could apply and overlap with the Advanced Sensor discussion.

The stakeholders identified a need for reference specimens that enable third-party *validation* of inspection technologies and technicians. This would enable greater confidence and justification for the use of existing NDE techniques that service industries provide. Again, many of these topics could have equally applied to the Advanced Sensors breakout session, but were raised here due to the desire for accurate conclusions from data obtained during inspections or periodic NDE investigations.

Evaluation combines needs in data mining and bridge management systems (BMS). Many state DOTs already perform element-level inspections, but methods for using data from these inspections are in need of refinement. First, routine visual inspections report obvious problems, but guidance in determining responses to problems is needed. For example, is a reported problem critical? Is the problem in a critical member? Has the growth of a crack relieved the stresses that produced it? Second, upon discovery of a problem in one bridge, what are the criteria for determining how comparable bridges with potentially similar problems should be investigated, and with what priority?

B. Presentations

Mike Loeffler (Bridge Operations and Maintenance, Ohio DOT) highlighted problems in determining the condition and the remaining load capacity of steel bridge pins. Determining whether the pins have frozen and should be considered fixed or whether they are they truly behaving as pins, are questions that sometimes remain unanswered. The limited capacity that results from corroded pins is illustrated by a particular bridge in Ohio. This bridge would have the capacity for two additional traffic lanes if the pins behaved as pins. However, the pins have seized, and the resulting analysis has shown that two lanes of traffic needed to be removed.

In another example, one pin was removed because NDE concluded that it was cracked. Upon removal, no crack was found. Yet another example, the load rating of one bridge in Ohio is governed by steel pins whose condition cannot be evaluated because of inaccessibility. The majority of a pin's surface is covered by the plates it connects, and so typically the ends are the only features that are visible. In some cases, the geometry of the connection is such that only one end of a pin is accessible.

D. Robert Hay (Waves in Solids LLC, State College, PA) presented an overview of (1) short-term monitoring systems of acoustic emission with associated strain that have been deployed by Waves in Solids LLC, (2) the role of these systems in risk-informed management of bridge maintenance, and (3) active (conventional) ultrasonic technology (UT) inspection methods.

George Hearn (Associate Professor, University of Colorado, Boulder) provided an introduction to the inspection discussion by pointing out different types of inspections, the motivation for any deviation in inspection intervals, and thresholds for decision making with reference to Connecticut, Oregon, and Michigan's inspection guidelines.

Sougata Roy (Senior Research Scientist, ATLSS Engineering Research Center, Lehigh University, Bethlehem, PA) presented an overview of orthotropic decks. Even though orthotropic decks can provide life spans exceeding 100 years and are considered an ABC technique, their implementation in the US is rare because of the high initial cost and potential for fatigue cracking if the fabrication quality is low. The most critical weld is the rib-to-deck weld because of its tight tolerances. Many fabricators do not want to specify a tighter tolerance weld because of the higher level of sample preparation, welder competence, and inspection required for that type of weld. A protocol for welds specific to orthotropic decks is desired, specifically distinguishing between a small versus a large discontinuity, as it would permit evaluation of what welds need to be repaired and which are acceptable. PAUT was highlighted as a potential NDE technique, but it requires standards and guidelines for use. The development of standard, consistent protocols, and guidelines for automated application would naturally fall within NIST's mission.

C. Discussion

The stakeholders identified fifteen bridge inspection topics during the breakout session. The first six are those topics that were deemed most important by the stakeholders and are listed in order of decreasing rankings in the final plenary vote.

1. Buried steel – determining location, size, and condition (corrosion) of concrete passive or prestressed reinforcement.

   Determining the size and condition of reinforcing steel in hardened concrete (including obsolete rebar types) is a measurement need. Older bars have different surface deformations (raised pattern) than modern bars. Very old bars are smooth. A new technology to see inside concrete elements must be proven on old bars, since their surfaces are so different. Bridge records would ideally consist of many items [American Association of State Highway and Transportation Officials 2008]; an illustrative selection of items for this discussion includes construction plans, shop drawings, as-built plans, specifications, and material certifications. The need for information on existence, location, type, and amount of buried steel in structures is not limited to older structures where construction plans and/or as-built drawings do not exist; it is also desired for younger structures for confirmation of current and future performance with calculations or justification for a proposed repair. Strands in post-tensioned members provide another venue for determination of the location and condition of inaccessible members.

2. Inspection reference specimens for validation of methods

   This discussion hinges around justification and confidence in many NDE techniques (particularly ground penetrating radar (GPR), PAUT, and UT) where the DOTs would like to provide more data to justify their preferred action. Standardized and certified visual output greatly improves the confidence of owners and ensures that the technicians employing the technique are interpreting it properly. Mike Loeffler's presentation illustrated the effect of not having accurate conclusions from NDE technologies. Development of reference specimens for buried as well as surface cracks was raised during the session. Another vein of this topic brought up the desire to automate or build in a post-processor for the output of some NDE techniques such that a qualified (yet not necessarily experienced) user would be able to make precise conclusions about the member's actual condition. The suggestion was to provide locations where NDE providers could obtain a third-party validation of their devices, setup, and conclusions. This idea fits well within NIST's mission to provide independent calibration, evaluation, and validation of measurement tools.

3. Visual inspection detection rates and validation

   Visual techniques dominate inspection methods defined in the NBIS. Inspections of fracture critical bridges consist of a very detailed visual inspection "that may be supplemented by nondestructive testing" [Electronic Code of Federal Regulations 2010]. FHWA published a report that showed that inspectors do not always satisfactorily locate or identify defects on reference specimens [Moore 2000]. Specific topics related to the visual inspection and probability of detection (POD) study were to define standards that defined a critical defect, the rate of detection relative to the defect's size (specifically of fatigue cracks), and the relation of critical defects to detectable defects. Studies of these topics could provide a basis for modification of existing inspector training courses.

4. Data mining applied to inspection data

    Analysis of data recorded from inspections (past data sets) offers the potential of optimizing maintenance effectiveness, scheduling, remaining life, and basic degradation rates. There is a need for employing inspection data (existing and new) in better software-based decision-aiding tools. Ideally, these applications would provide interfaces with existing software for ease of use.

5. Steel pins and rivets—methods for condition determination and validation of conclusions

    Although pin and rivet connections do not dominate new construction, certain classes of bridges in the existing inventory contain large quantities of these connections, which are sometimes inaccessible and, therefore, difficult to inspect. Methods are needed for determining the condition of these connections, including quantifying section losses in connections with multiple plies.

6. Validation methods for training received

    This topic is very similar to topic 3 with the slight distinction of focusing more on the ability of the inspector, rather than the type of defect, and external factors that may affect identification and description of problem areas.

7. Corrosion

    Existing devices that detect and characterize corrosion need to be validated. Magnesium chloride ($MgCl_2$) is known to aggravate the corrosion of steel members, so standards for material performance and rates of corrosion that account for various de-icing programs and the local climate are also desired. Magnesium chloride has replaced sodium chloride at some DOTs, and road sand replaces it at some others. Any salt is bad for bridge steel, but sodium chloride (NaCl) has been thought by some to be more harmful than $MgCl_2$. In Colorado, road sand has contributed substantially to particulate pollution (as measured by the P10 indicator of air quality). Therefore, Colorado DOT has reduced its use of sand and, correspondingly, increased its use of $MgCl_2$, even though salt is detrimental to bridges. The ability to measure the corrosion of buried steel elements, such as steel straps in MSE walls and rock bolts, was also mentioned.

8. Standards for inspecting inaccessible or poorly accessible elements are desired to guide procedures for sampling, destructive testing, and replacement.

    Scour is the most frequent cause of bridge collapse, but inspection of scour damage is difficult, because of lack of visibility and stressful inspection situations (difficult and sometimes hazardous underwater working conditions for divers). Therefore, guidance on inspection of underwater piers is needed, so that it can be performed in the most effective and timely manner. A review of existing technologies for detection and monitoring of scour, leading to guidelines for bridge owners, was also suggested.

9. Monitoring

Standards that extend Florida DOT's work on long-term monitoring of cracks in steel and the provision of artifacts that can be used for calibration of crack lengths and expected growth rates are desired. This applies both to surface and buried cracks. Monitoring of the remaining population of bridges (or elements) of the same type after a failure was suggested as a measurement and data need.

10. There is a need to validate load capacity determination with sensor technologies and FEM, which includes appropriate boundary conditions and the stress history of the bridge.

11. Validation of techniques that determine the condition of inner plies of steel connections (gusset plates) is needed.

12. Field measurements of total and residual stresses.

One application for the absolute stress device would be distinguishing between distortion-induced stress and direct stress. Growth in the distortion-induced stress may exhaust the spare capacity in the original design.

13. Potential for monitoring movement of structures with a more accurate GPS-type device (with millimeter resolution) was suggested.

14. Metrology is needed for determining the depths of unknown foundations.

15. Metrology is needed for determining the effects of multiple applications of heatstraightening on the material locally and the bridge globally.

II. Advanced Sensors
A. Introduction
The principal foci of the Advanced Sensors session were the development, standardization, and validation of sensors, data transmission/compression, and data analysis/interpretation for long-term and short-term monitoring of bridges. Other closely related topics discussed in these sessions overlapped with those in the session on Uncertainty in Inspection Information, and these included the development and validation of devices and methods for periodic NDE investigation of bridge components.

B. Presentations
Catherine French (I.T. Distinguished Professor, Department of Civil Engineering, University of Minnesota, Minneapolis) reviewed the permanent instrumentation, data acquisition, and structural modeling of the new I-35W St. Anthony Falls Bridge. The University of Minnesota is responsible for sensor-data collection and interpretation over the first three years and for development of a long-term monitoring system.

Larry Olson (Olson Engineering, Wheat Ridge, CO) reviewed impact-echo methods and laser-based methods employed by Olson Engineering to characterize concrete delamination and bridge deflection, respectively.

C. Discussion

The stakeholders identified fourteen technical areas in which research would serve to advance SHM of bridges. The first seven of these areas are listed in the order of their ranking in the final plenary session.

1. Absolute and residual stress measurements and reference specimens

   A number of types of sensors are currently commercially available or in the process of being developed for measuring changes in quasi-static strain relative to that at the time of installation of the sensor. However, methods are not established for accurate and cost-effective field measurements of absolute stress or strain, and such data are desired for determining how close metals are to their yield point. In the absence of such metrology, the initial state of stress in new bridges can only be estimated from the design, unless initial stresses in the unloaded stage are measured with permanently mounted sensors during the entire construction process. In older bridges, engineering estimates of stress based on the design generally have large margins of uncertainty, because of unknown structural history, such as settling of piers and impact damage. To address this situation, NIST could perform research on methods for absolute-stress measurements in the field and develop artifacts for validation of methods.

2. Environmental and aging effects on sensors for long-term monitoring

   New bridges are designed to have lifetimes of many decades, but no sensors currently being installed for structural monitoring have been tested over such long periods of time. This raises questions about whether such sensors will survive and provide reliable data over the lifetime of a bridge. For example, measurements provided by vibrating-wire strain gages on the new I-35W bridge are dependent on the tension of the metallic wires, which may drift over time because of relaxation of the wires. NIST could potentially provide impartial research and evaluation of such degradation, leading to standardized accelerated-test procedures.

3. Standard testing apparatus (test beds) for SHM technologies

   No mechanisms or standards exist for impartial validation of the performance of many new SHM technologies. This places end users, such as state DOT engineers, in the difficult position of deciding on the usefulness of committing great long-term resources to the deployment of technologies that have been validated only by the manufacturers with non-standardized tests. To address this situation, NIST could develop and house standardized apparatus for evaluating SHM sensors and instrumentation. This apparatus could include testbeds with elements that are either destroyed during the tests (for example, with known time-dependent fatigue damage) or that remain constant (for example, with known static strain, curvature, displacement, vibrational modes, or defects).

4. Corrosion sensors

Corrosion of steel reinforcements and prestressing strands is a major cause of structural deterioration of reinforced concrete bridges. Because such corrosion occurs at internal material interfaces, it cannot be detected through visual inspection. Therefore, the development of sensors for detecting and characterizing the extent and rate of corrosion is a high priority.

5. Calibration acceptance and rejection criteria

Data obtained from NDE inspection can be complex and difficult to interpret on real structures in the field, and this leads to ill-defined acceptance/rejection criteria. An example of this is phased-array ultrasonic testing (PAUT), which provides information on discontinuities within structural components in the form of spatial maps. NIST could help to resolve this problem by establishing calibration methods and systematic methods for evaluating data.

6. Micro-electro-mechanical systems (MEMS) or other low-cost technologies that measure acceleration, strain, or displacement

The costs of sensors and instrumentation for processing sensor data are major obstacles to the practical realization of widespread SHM of bridges. MEMS offer particularly great promise for reducing costs and associated complexity of mechanical sensing and signal processing through wafer-level fabrication and integration of electronics. A potential role of NIST in this area is the invention and development of MEMS or other low-cost sensors for characterizing acceleration, quasi-static and/or dynamic strain, large-scale displacement, or local displacement.

7. Frameworks for sensor selection and placement

Determining an approach for efficient and cost-effective deployment of SHM sensors on a structure can be a complex process, involving an analysis of principal structural vulnerabilities and related properties/parameters, and, from these, selection of optimal sensor types and their placement. The broad expertise and impartial perspective of NIST place it in position where it could effectively help establish guidelines for sensor selection and placement.

8. Sensors for alkali-silica reaction (ASR)

ASR is a chemical reaction between the cement and aggregate of concrete that causes expansion and cracking. Microscopy techniques are employed in the laboratory to detect such reaction, but detection in the field, before obvious structural degradation, is much more challenging. New, inexpensive, fast, easy, and reliable methods for early detection of ASR in the field are required to enable early mitigation of weakened bridges [Cooley 2006].

9. Wireless, robust, self-powered sensors with on-board processing

The cost of installing wiring to power sensors on bridges is a major impediment to widespread deployment of networks for structural health monitoring. The cost and complexity of processing large amounts of data from such sensing networks are also impediments. Wireless sensors with on-board data processing could overcome these problems. However, currently available wireless sensors are limited with respect to their robustness and battery life. Therefore, the development of new sensors with long-term reliability, self-sustaining power, and integrated data processing (minimizing the volume and complexity of transmitted data) is a high priority.

10. Sensing of fatigue cracks

Monitoring the initiation, growth, and state of fatigue cracks in steel is required for effective risk-based assessment of priorities for bridge repairs or replacement. Various approaches, ranging from periodic visual inspection to short-term acoustic-emission sensing, have been pursued, but none has been demonstrated to provide a reliable and cost-effective long-term solution. Practical sensors and associated electronics and algorithms for signal- and data-processing are needed for long-term unattended monitoring of fatigue cracks.

11. Data-compression methods

Digital processing and analysis of large volumes of data generated by hundreds (or, potentially, thousands) of sensors in a network on a bridge are major challenges. Therefore, developing methods and establishing protocols for data compression is a high priority.

12. Protocols for networking and communication of sensor arrays specific to bridges

Standards for sensor network structure, in relation to the hierarchy and paths of communication and the format of transmitted data, are not established. Differing opinions on this topic were expressed at the workshop. On the one hand, NIST, as an impartial agency with expertise in information technology, could expedite progress in this technical area, with a focus on nonproprietary algorithms and code. On the other hand, an NDE supplier expressed the opinion that technical advances in this field would best be developed privately, because users are already employing commercially produced algorithms and related instrumentation that overcome some of the networking challenges

13. Tools for data interpretation

Methods of data interpretation, including modeling strategies and algorithms, are not fully established or standardized for either NDE inspection or new SHM sensor networks. NIST would play a useful role by developing analytical tools and establishing guidelines for choosing approaches to the analysis of specific types of measurements.

14. Guidelines for structural health monitoring of new bridges, starting with construction

Uncertainty in the quantification of the mechanical state of new bridges is introduced by incomplete or indirect information on initial dead-load conditions (stress or strain in the absence of applied traffic load). Rather than relying on engineering calculations of stresses and strains based on the idealized bridge design, it is preferable to obtain direct measurements that serve as a baseline for subsequent time- and load-dependent sensor data. An appropriate role for NIST in this area may be to provide guidelines for monitoring strain during the process of construction. New bridge construction is increasingly focused on accelerated bridge construction (ABC) methods, which are dominated by prefabricated concrete sections. Therefore, any approach for obtaining baseline sensor data during construction must address these techniques and materials.

III. Behavior of Connections

A. Introduction

This summary documents the discussion in the Tuesday and Wednesday breakout sessions. Some background material has been added that did not appear in the discussion. Much of this information is referenced to research results and documents that the participants mentioned during the discussion.

At the close of the session, the participants reviewed the potential research areas that they had raised during the discussion. The research topics naturally fell into three groups: (1) timely, important, and NIST-suitable; (2) important but not suited for NIST research areas; and (3) not discussed in detail. After selecting the first group, the stakeholders voted by show of hands on the importance of each topic within the group.

B. Presentations

Karl Frank (Hirschfeld Industries, Austin, Texas, recently retired from the University of Texas at Austin) reviewed connection design and construction issues, including the need for a new mid-strength bolt, the use of epoxy bearing bolts and fillers, and galvanizing-treatment effects on weld cracking.

Todd Helwig (University of Texas at Austin) reviewed the effects of cross-frame connections on bridges with skewed supports and construction difficulties with bridges with curved girder systems.

Arturo Schultz (University of Minnesota) presented research on structural health monitoring for response modification of bridges.

C. Discussion

The stakeholders identified six research areas that were deemed timely, important, and potentially suited for NIST research. They are listed below in descending order of significance as ranked during the final plenary session by the stakeholders.

1. Methods to rapidly determine load rating of bridges

    An on-going problem is determining the load rating for new and existing bridges. The discussion of this research area ranged quite widely. Participants were clear that methods that used strain gages on bridges were not rapid. They did include the possibility of using a diagnostic load test. One participant speculated that the ideal system for producing a bridge's load rating would be able to take a photo, digitize it, and input the results to an analysis tool. The methods need to be simple and robust, so much so that a "guy from the county department" can use them. Another opined that low-cost meant the ability to characterize twenty bridges per day. Another possibility would be to use methods that monitored the ambient vibration level by use of the live load of the bridge itself.

    Apparently, the Army Corps of Engineers is conducting similar research devoted to rapid rating of bridges for force projection, due to the weight of military equipment (Chowdhury and Ray,

2003). Ian Friedland pointed out that a FHWA project exists in this area (NCHRP 12-78 scheduled to be completed 3/2/2010).

Fuchs described an existing FHWA program to implement a laser system that could measure bridge deflections during fabrication [Fuchs 2004]. The discussion in the breakout session centered on the entire laser system. This system would have the capability to determine the actual load rating without reference to the original plans.

2. Improved crack-arrest strategies

Two separate issues were joined in the discussion of this area: (i) dynamic fracture toughness requirements to incorporate crack arrest in design of fracture critical members, and (ii) better ways to arrest fatigue cracks, supported by more experimental results, especially for distortion-induced cracks.

The advent of high-performance steels (HPS) with enhanced toughness may provide crack-arrest capability in fracture critical members. Wright has discussed potential application of high-performance steels and the FHWA perspective [Wright 2002]. Development of toughness requirements coupled with large size tests to validate performance in welded fabricated girders would accelerate the use of HPS. The payoff would be reduced inspection costs when higher-strength steel requires fewer members Distortion-induced cracking is the most prevalent form of cracking in steel bridges. Bridges built through the 1970's contain numerous locations susceptible to this form of fatigue cracking. The cracks form where differential displacements of the structure elements are concentrated in local gaps between connection elements. Typically, these are slow-growing fatigue cracks that initially are no cause for concern. However, as they grow, the cracks can turn and become normal to the bending stress in the girders. Reliable methods of arresting these cracks are needed. Traditionally, hole drilling at the crack tip followed in some cases by the insertion of a tightened high-strength bolt has been used. This and other techniques have not always been successful. A fracture mechanics analysis of existing and new techniques is needed. The results should be verified by laboratory and field studies.

3 Methods for inspecting multiple plies for corrosion

A method for detecting corrosion underneath multiple-ply plates, such as are found in gusset plates, would be extremely useful. Current ultrasonic methods are defeated by the reflections from the interfaces between the plates. Ian Friedland pointed out that the FHWA Turner-Fairbank Research center is currently evaluating two commercial methods for identifying buried corrosion.

4. Methods for determining bolt pretension

Methods for determining the bolt tension in a connection in the field could help assess the condition of connections. Some participants noted that the existing, commercial ultrasonic devices required the bolts to be machined at both ends, and that this requirement made the devices cost-prohibitive. An affordable device could also be useful for rivets. Many existing bridges use riveted, rather than bolted, connections.

Existing, commercial ultrasonic strategies typically use length measurements made ultrasonically before and after tightening. These methods may also require specially prepared bolts. Some research already exists on methods that do not require the bolt to be measured beforehand. These use the difference between shear and pressure waves to determine the actual stress state in the bolt [Jhang 2006, Kim 2009, Toda 2000, Walaszek 2006]. Some of these use electromagnetic (EMAT) instead of piezoelectric transducers. It is not clear what field-performance tests have been completed, and how effective the technique is on real bolts.

5.   Retrofits for cable hangers for fire protection

The anchorages for suspenders in suspension bridges and cable hangers in arch bridges are vulnerable to fire at the deck level, for example, from a tanker fire [Zoli 2007]. The socket is attached to the wire rope by brooming out the ends of the wire rope and potting them in either molten zinc or epoxy. Zinc melts at approximately 400 °C, and epoxy is limited to about 200 °C. Little data exists on the strength degradation of epoxy with temperature. The issue extends beyond suspension bridges, since cable-stayed bridges, stadiums, and glass-wall buildings all use socketed cables or wire ropes. These structures have high occupancy, and failure could lead to large loss of life. Methods to retrofit these existing systems to improve their reliability at elevated temperatures are needed as well as development of new systems that are not vulnerable during a fire. Furthermore, the research could take advantage of a unique NIST facility, the 35 MN tensile test machine on the Gaithersburg campus (53 MN in compression, 35 MN in tension).

6.   Acoustic Emission

Although the participants acknowledged that a separate breakout session was devoted to inspection strategies, they chose to discuss acoustic emission characterization, as it related to connections. They identified four areas of particular concern: (1) developing lower-cost sensors, (2) improving signal processing of AE signals, (3) developing new or improved communication protocols for *ad hoc* networks, and (4) developing improved accept/reject criteria for what constitutes a non-noise signal.

IV. Mechanical Response of Materials
A. Introduction

This summary documents the discussion in the Tuesday and Wednesday breakout sessions.

At the close of each session, the stakeholders reviewed the potential research areas that they had raised during the discussion. The research topics naturally fell into three groups: (1) timely, important, and NIST-suitable; (2) important but not suited for NIST research areas; and (3) not discussed in detail. After selecting the first group, the stakeholders voted by show of hands on the importance of each topic, and selected the top five to present during the final plenary session.

B. Presentations

Theodore Zoli (HNTB) presented a broad overview of the topic of bridge failure due to extreme events. Truss bridges are overrepresented in bridge failures in the US (defined as inability to carry live loads, not necessarily catastrophic). Flooding is a more frequent cause of damage than scour. Impact often renders many truss bridges unstable, but collapse is rare, fortunately, because typically bridge columns are designed for impact, although bridge decks are not. In AASHTO LRFD (Load and Resistance Factor Design), non-redundant bridges are designed for only 5 % more load than redundant bridges. A bridge failure database is needed.

Dennis Mertz (University of Delaware) commented briefly on the need to clarify the difference between a subjective description of a bridge condition (used for allocation of funds) and load rating by testing (that has little to say about actual failure). He further discussed the measured behavior of a structure versus the calculated behavior based on the overdesign for safety. He pointed out the need to understand the uncertainties and assumptions for all of these measurements and designs.

Todd Helwig (University of Texas Austin) reviewed issues associated with curved girder design and erection modeling. He pointed out the need to understand how certain reports define "failure."

C. Discussion

The stakeholders identified eight research needs, described below in descending order of significance as indicated by votes during the final plenary session (not as ranked in the breakout session).

1.   Resistance to fire

The behavior of high performance steel (HPS) at temperatures ranging between 400 °C and 1100 °C needs to be better defined for use in design and analysis.

Fires from tanker trucks present a danger to bridges. Guidance is needed for bridge design, repair, and replacement, as well as fire-fighting strategies (cooling the fire, particularly steel members with water, evacuating the bridge, commitment of fire-fighting personnel, etc.). It usually takes two hours before a tanker truck fire can be brought under control. Double-deck bridges are particularly vulnerable, as tanker accidents, spills and fires can occur on the lower deck, thus exposing the upper deck to flames. Asphalt pavement can do more than burn; it can also act as a sponge for fuel.

The Throgs Neck Bridge fire is an example of fire damage on deep girders with thin webs (slenderness ratio approaching 200) whose strength after a moderate-temperature wood fire was difficult to evaluate because of web buckling. Thin webs are much more difficult to straighten than flanges. Guidance is also needed as to how many times one can heat-straighten steel before the properties of the steel are changed. In another example, a coconut fire under a cable bridge ignited the anti-corrosion layer around the cable, exposing a significant vulnerability.

The behavior of connections in fires also needs to be better understood, in particular the fatigue resistance of bolted and riveted connections, especially when they are loose or exposed to high temperatures. Connections are typically not designed for member over-strength (that is, connected members fail before the connection itself fails).

2.   Size (scale) effects

The strength of structural members and connections is determined by small-scale tests, which are not always a faithful representation of full-size behavior. The problem has been studied for reinforced concrete members in shear, but is not limited to that. The full-scale tests of steel gusset plates at FHWA present a unique opportunity to study this problem for steel connections (NCHRP Project 12-84 "Gusset Plate Connections for Steel Bridges").

3.   Load rating, structural deterioration, and monitoring

Changes in emphasis on resilience, robustness, and safety require a reconsideration of load rating, which is based on calculations, not necessarily in accordance with physical measurements. The problem of scour of bridge piers, in particular, requires better modeling and measurements.

We need a better understanding of the fatigue resistance of bolted and riveted connections, especially when they are loose or exposed to high temperatures. Connections are assumed to be stronger than the members they connect, but are typically not designed for member over-strength.

4.   Resistance to impact

Most impacts on bridges are caused by trucks whose height exceeds clearance, but barge impacts on bridge piers, or even impacts caused by a weather-induced event, are possible. (For example, on 29 August 2005, Hurricane Katrina pushed the offshore platform PEMEX's PSS Chemul, a 13,000 t semisubmersible accommodation unit that was under renovation, and wedged it under the Cochrane Bridge in Mobile, Alabama.) We also need better understanding of high strain rate effects. Train and vehicular impacts usually occur at speeds below 90 m/s (200 mi/h), but the fighter jet that cut the cables of a funicular in Italy was traveling at more than 270 m/s (600 mi/h). Flying objects set in motion by an explosion range in speed from 180 m/s (400 mi/h) to 610 m/s (1320 mi/h).

Instrumenting a bridge before explosive demolition is an attractive way to better understand progressive collapse and the behavior of members and connections under dynamic loads.

5.   NDE for corrosion detection below protective coatings or plies

Corrosion and fatigue are perennial problems for steel bridges. The measurement of section loss due to corrosion in steel plates of multiple plies is a problem in bad need of solution. It is also desirable to be able to monitor by NDE the condition of the structure through protective coatings.

6.   Dynamic behavior of bridge cables

We need to better understand the dynamic behavior of cable anchors on suspension bridges. Are we under-predicting wind forces against bridges, especially flutter? Cables also retain memory of the capstan used to draw them (typical diameter 1.5 m (5 ft)), and their cracking can often be traced to the curvature of the capstan.

If hydrogen embrittlement can be alleviated, galvanizing prestressing cables may be an attractive way to resist corrosion.

7.   New fabrication processes

Explosive forming is used in making machine parts, but not bridge components and connections. Why not? Also, friction-stir welding needs to be investigated for use on bridges.

8.   Concrete

Various issues were identified: early age cracking, transverse cracking of decks, cement replacement (to reduce carbon footprint), thermal control for mass concrete, and difficulties in slip forming.

Bibliography

American Association of State Highway and Transportation Officials. (2008). *The Manual for Bridge Evaluation*. Washington, DC: AASHTO Publications.

Chase, S. B. (2005). The role of sensing and measurement in achieving FHWA's strategic vision for highway infrastructure. In F. Ansari (Ed.), *Sensing Issues in Civil Structural Health Monitoring*. (pp. 23- 32). Netherlands. Springer.

Chase, S. B. & Laman, J. A. (2000). Dynamics and Field Testing of Bridges. *Transportation in the new millennium: state of the art and future directions*. Retrieved 21 June 2010. http://onlinepubs.trb.org/onlinepubs/millennium/00029.pdf

Chowdhury, M. R. and Ray, J. C. (2003). Accelerometers for bridge load testing, US Army Engineering Research and Development Center, Vicksburg, MS 39180-6199, NDT&E International 36 237–244.

Cooley, A. & Brumfield, J. W. (2006). ASR Benchmark Workshop. *Federal Highway Administration*. Retrieved 22 June 2010, from http://www.fhwa.dot.gov/pavement/concrete/asrbench.pdf

Electronic Code of Federal Regulations. (2010). Retrieved 1 July 2010 from http://ecfr.gpoaccess.gov/cgi/t/text/text-idx?c=ecfr&sid=86dce31d4371c549d6fcfbbb8beefd56&rgn=div6&view=text&node=23:1.0.1.7.28.3&idno=23

Fisher, J., Kulak, G. L., & Smith, I. F. C. (1998). National Steel Bridge Alliance. *A Fatigue Primer for Structural Engineers*. Retrieved 18 June 2010 from http://www.aisc.org/store/p-1590-a-fatigue-primert-for-structural-engineers.aspx

Friedland, I. (Speaker). (2010). Every Day Counts [Audiovisual presentation]. AASHTO Bridge Meeting, Sacramento, CA.

Friedland, I. (2010). Personal e-mail, 8 June 2010.

Fuchs, P. A., Washer, G. A., Chase, S. B., & Moore, M. (2004). Laser-based instrumentation for bridge load testing. *Journal of Performance of Constructed Facilities.* 18(4). 213-219.

Hartman, J. (Speaker). (2010). NCHRP 12-84 Gusset Plate Connections for Steel Bridges Update [Audiovisual presentation]. AASHTO Bridge Meeting, Sacramento, CA.

Jhang, K. Y. & Quan, H. H. & Ha, J. & Kim, N. Y. (2006). Estimation of clamping force in high-tension bolts through ultrasonic velocity measurement. *Ultrasonics.* 44. E1339-E1342.

Kim, N. & Hong, M. (2009). Measurement of axial stress using mode-converted ultrasound. *NDT & E International.* 42(3). 164-169.

Klein, T. W. (2007). Cable assemblies in the 21st century. In *Proceedings of the 2007 World Steel Bridge Symposium.* Retrieved 18 May 2010 from
http://www.aisc.org/WorkArea/linkit.aspx?LinkIdentifier=id&ItemID=20606

Moore, M., Phares, B., Graybeal, B., Rolander, D., & Washer, G. (2000). Reliability of Visual Inspection for Highway Bridges. Federal Highway Administration. Retrieved 1 July 2010 from
http://www.tfhrc.gov/hnr20/nde/pdfs/01021a.pdf

NCHRP 12-78, Evaluation of Load Rating by Load and Resistance Factor Rating. Retrieved 26 July 2010 from
http://144.171.11.40/cmsfeed/TRBNetProjectDisplay.asp?ProjectID=1629

Toda, H., Go, Y., Yokoyama, K., Yosikawa, O., &Yawata T. (2000). Measurement of axial-stress in high-tension bolts by acoustoelastic velocity-ratio method. In Uomoto, T. (Ed.), *Non-destructive Testing in Civil Engineering 2000 – Seiken Symposium No. 26.* 109-115.

Transportation Pooled Fund Program – TPF. (2010). Retrieved 22 June 2010 from
http://www.pooledfund.org/browse.asp?action-study_number

Walaszek, H. & Bouteille, P. (2006). Ultrasonic stress measurement: Application to preload assessment on already tightened bolts. In Reimbers, W. & Quander, S. (Eds.), *Residual Stresses VII Materials Science Forum.* 524-525. 459-464.

Wright, W. J. (2002). Fracture toughness requirements for highway bridges: past and future trends. *Progress in Structural Engineering and Materials.* 4(1). 96-104.

Yoneyama, S., Kitagawa, A., Iwata, S., Tani, K., & Kikuta, H. (2007). Bridge deflection measurement using digital image correlation. *Experimental Techniques.* 31(1). 34-40.

Zoli, T. P. & Steinhouse, J. (2007). Some considerations in the design of long span bridges against progressive collapse. *23th US-Japan Bridge Engineering Workshop.* Tsukuba, Japan. Retrieved 22 June 2010 from
http://www.pwri.go.jp/eng/ujnr/tc/g/pdf/23/23-2-3zoli.pdf

Appendix I – Presentations

I. Keynote Presentations

II. Breakout Session Presentations

III. Supplemental Information

(These presentations are only on the CD version of the report.)

Appendix II – Agenda

**National Institute of
Standards and Technology**
U.S. Department of Commerce

Workshop on Quantitative Tools for Condition Assessment of Aging Infrastructure

Dates: May 4 and 5, 2010

Location: NIST, Boulder, CO

Purpose

This workshop is designed to sharpen the focus of NIST's Materials Science and Engineering Laboratory (MSEL) programs by matching the measurement technology capabilities of MSEL with existing technology gaps in the realm of assessing bridge performance to prioritize their repair and replacement. The workshop will include approximately 30 stakeholders from universities, professional societies, industry, and the DOTs (state and federal departments of transportation). The stakeholders will help NIST researchers identify areas that would provide the best application of their skills and to propose potential partners for specific projects. The workshop will start with several keynote presentations to frame the topics, followed by parallel breakout sessions to develop and rank potential research activities. The workshop will conclude with all the stakeholders to develop a consensus and prioritized list.

We have identified four tentative topic areas: uncertainty in inspection information, advanced sensors, behavior of connections, and materials mechanical response.

Output

The meeting will develop a ranked list of activities that MSEL staff could perform in support of the nation's bridge infrastructure. The results will be published as a NIST Internal Report, and circulated within the bridge industry to find partners in our activities.

Scope

See separate document.

Steering committee

Frank Gayle, Stephanie Hooker, William Luecke, Tom Siewert

Organizing committee

Stephanie Hooker, Mark Iadicola, Dave McColskey, Tom Siewert, Jessica Terry, Dat Duthinh, Ward Johnson

Schedule

Tues	May 4
8:00	Arrive at the Visitor Center at 325 Broadway, Boulder, CO Receive badge and parking permit, proceed to the north of Building 1 for parking, enter east door at the front of Building 1 (faces Broadway) and proceed to room 1107 for light refreshments
8:30	**Welcome** Tom Siewert, Project Leader, Materials Reliability Division
8:35	**NIST Overview: Organization and Mission** Frank Gayle, Metallurgy Division Chief
8:50	**Overview of MSEL Plan: Quantitative Tools for Condition Assessment of Aging Infrastructure** Stephanie Hooker, Materials Reliability Division Chief
9:30	**Keynote:** *Bridge Research: Current Issues and Future Opportunities* Ian Friedland, Technical Director, Bridges and Structures R&D, FHWA
10:15	**Break**
10:30	**Keynote: Research Perspective, Overview and Measurement Gaps that MSEL might fill** Dan Frangopol, Fazlur R. Khan Endowed Chair of Structural Engineering and Architecture, Assessing and predicting the performance of bridges to prioritize their repair and replacement: accomplishments and challenges
11:15	**Keynote: AISI Bridge Task Force, Overview and Measurement Gaps that MSEL might fill** Alex Wilson, Customer Service Technical Manager, ArcelorMittal
12:00	**Lunch**
1:15	**Role of Breakout Sessions** Tom Siewert
1:30	**Breakout sessions** Room 1107 Uncertainty in Inspection Information Leader: George Hearn, Recorder: Jessica Terry Contributions from • George Hearn, Overview of inspection information issues • Mike Loeffler, Degradation rates, database for new materials • Sougata Roy, Improved inspection methods for orthotropic deck fabrication Room 1103/5 Materials Mechanical Response Leader: Theodore Zoli, Recorder: Dat Duthinh Contributions from • Theodore Zoli, Overview of mechanical response issues • Todd Helwig, Curved plate girder design • Dennis Mertz, Steel bridge evaluation
3:30	**Break**
3:45	**Breakout Sessions** Room 1107 Advanced Sensors Leader: Steve Lovejoy, Recorder: Ward Johnson Contributions from • Steven Lovejoy, SHM of bridges • Catherine French, I-35W Sensors Room 1103/5 Behavior of Connections Leader: Karl Frank, Recorder: William Luecke Contributions from • Karl Frank, Overview of connection issues • Art Schultz, SHM of gusset plates in FC bridges
5:45	**Meeting Adjourns**

Weds	May 5
8:30	**Resume Breakout Sessions** Room 1107 Uncertainty in Inspection Information Leader: George Hearn, Recorder: Jessica Terry Contributions from: • Mike Loeffler, Test standards for large steel pin testing Room 1103/5 Materials Mechanical Response Leader: Theodore Zoli, Recorder: Dat Duthinh Contributions from: • Dennis Mertz, Redundancy in steel bridges • Art Schultz, Enhanced safety of bridges
9:30	**Breakout Sessions** Room 1107 Advanced Sensors Leader: Steve Lovejoy, Recorder: Ward Johnson Contributions from: • Steven Lovejoy, Fatigue and fracture of bridges • Catherine French, Consideration for the development of real-time dynamic testing using servo-hydraulic actuation Room 1103/5 Behavior of Connections Leader: Karl Frank, Recorder: William Luecke Contributions from: • Karl Frank, Fatigue strength of welded cruciform joints • Todd Helwig, Cross-frame connections effect on steel bridges with skewed supports • Sougata Roy, Fatigue critical details in orthotropic decks
10:30	**Break**
10:45	**Report Conclusions and Action Items** Tom Siewert Uncertainty in Inspection Information Behavior of Connections Advanced Sensors Materials Mechanical Response
11:30	**General Discussion and Closing** Tom Siewert
12:00	**Lunch**
1:30	**MSEL Tours:** • Materials Labs in Boulder • Atomic Clock, Building 1 • Bulk Mechanical Testing Facilities, Building 2 • Mechanical Testing and Pressurized Hydrogen, Building 12 • Steel recovered from Big Thompson Canyon bridges, Building 8

Appendix III – Topic Rankings

Stakeholders were each given six votes to be distributed in whatever categories or weighting they chose, with the possibility of multiple votes from any individual for any topic. The voting stakeholders included: five bridge owners, eleven university researchers, and nine industry personnel. The rankings are ordered according to the total number of stakeholders' votes.

	Topic	Bridge Owners	University	Industry	Total
1.	Sensors – absolute and residual stress measurements and reference specimens	8	6	4	18
2.	Connections – methods to rapidly determine load rating of bridges	2	6	4	12
3.	Connections – improved crack-arrest strategies	3	4	3	10
4.	Inspection – buried steel; determine location, size, and condition (corrosion) of concrete reinforcement; determine location, force and condition (corrosion) in prestressing steel	3	4	3	10
5.	Sensors – environmental and aging effects on sensors for long-term monitoring	0	5	4	9
6.	Inspection – inspection reference specimens for validation of methods	2	3	4	9
7.	Inspection – visual inspection detection rates and validation	1	6	1	8
8.	Sensors – standard testing apparatus (test beds) for SHM technologies	1	3	4	8
9.	Material Response – resistance to fire	2	2	3	7
10.	Material Response – size (scale) effects	1	3	3	7
11.	Material Response – load rating, structural deterioration, and monitoring	1	4	2	7
12.	Inspection – data mining applied to inspection data	0	5	1	6
13.	Sensors – corrosion sensors	1	2	3	6
14.	Connections – methods for inspecting multiple plies for corrosion	3	1	2	6
15.	Connections – methods for determining bolt pretension	0	3	2	5
16.	Sensors – calibration acceptance and rejection criteria	0	2	3	5
17.	Material Response – resistance to impact	0	4	1	5
18.	Inspection – steel pins and rivets; methods for condition determination and validation of conclusions	1	1	2	4
19.	Connections – retrofits for cable hangers for fire protection	0	2	1	3

	Topic	Bridge Owners	University	Industry	Total
20.	Sensors – MEMS or other low-cost technologies that measure acceleration, strain, or displacement	1	0	2	3
21.	Sensors – frameworks for sensor selection and placement	0	0	1	1
22.	Material Response – NDE for corrosion detection below protective coatings or plies	0	0	1	1
23.	Inspection – validation methods for training received	0	0	0	0

Appendix IV a – Stakeholders

Anderson, Jeffrey	Colorado DOT
Atadero, Rebecca	Colorado State University
Connor, Robert	Purdue University
ElSafty, Adel	University of North Florida
Frangopol, Dan	Lehigh University
Frank, Karl	Hirschfeld Industries
French, Catherine	University of Minnesota
Friedland, Ian	FHWA
Goldstein, Neil	JenTek Sensors
Hay, D Robert	Waves in Solids, LLC
Hearn, George	University of Colorado
Helwig, Todd	University of Texas
Lane, Susan	PCA
Loeffler, Michael	Ohio DOT
Lovejoy, Steven	Oregon DOT
McEleney, William	NSBA
Merritt, James	PHMSA/DOT
Mertz, Dennis	Delaware University
Mulligan, Denis	Golden Gate Bridge, Highway and Transportation District
Nowak, Andy	University of Nebraska, Lincoln
Olson, Larry	Olson Engineering
Piazza, Mark	Pipeline Research Council International, Inc
Roy, Sougata	Lehigh University
Schultz, Arturo	University of Minnesota
Sinha, Sunil	Virginia Tech
Snyder, Dan	AISI
Verma, Krishna	FHWA
Wilson, Alex	ArcelorMittal/AISI Bridge Task Force
Zavattieri, Pablo	Purdue University
Zoli, Theodore	HNTB

Appendix IV b – NIST Participants

Baker-Jarvis, James	Electromagnetics Division
Drexler, Elizabeth	Materials Reliability Division
Duthinh, Dat	Metallurgy Division
Fekete, James	Materials Reliability Division
Gayle, Frank	Metallurgy Division
Hamstad, Marvin	Materials Reliability Division
Hooker, Stephanie	Materials Reliability Division
Iadicola, Mark	Metallurgy Division
Johnson, Ward	Materials Reliability Division
Luecke, William	Metallurgy Division
McColskey, David	Materials Reliability Division
McCowan, Chris	Materials Reliability Division
Richards, Mark	Materials Reliability Division
Siewert, Tom	Materials Reliability Division
Sowards, Jeffrey	Materials Reliability Division
Surek, Jack	Electromagnetics Division
Terry, Jessica	Materials Reliability Division
Weeks, Timothy	Materials Reliability Division

www.ingramcontent.com/pod-product-compliance
Lightning Source LLC
Chambersburg PA
CBHW080355290526
45791CB00009BA/2880